I AM A MAN
BUT I AM
NOT A
CHAUVINIST

101 ACTIONS OF A
WISE MAN

Published by Mattyson Media an imprint of MAMM
Matthew Ashimolowo Media Ministries
57 Waterden Road
Hackney Wick
London
E15 2EE

Bible quotes are from the King James Bible
unless otherwise stated.
ISBN 1 874 646-35-X

Printed in Great Britain by
Clays Ltd, St Ives plc

101 ACTIONS OF A WISE MAN

Wise men are not carried away by looks.

*Lust not after her beauty in thine heart; neither let her take
thee with her eyelids.*
Proverbs 6:25 (KJV)

*Favour is deceitful, and beauty is vain: but a woman that
feareth the LORD, she shall be praised.*
Proverbs 31:30 (KJV)

Beauty is said to be in the eye of the beholder. Men
oftentimes are easily carried away by what a woman
looks like on the outside. They draw their
conclusions and decide to pursue.

A godly and a wise man would recognise the fact
that looks can be deceptive and misleading. Though
beauty may be in the eye of the beholder, beauty is
also a matter of interpretation. What to one is
attractive, may for another be repulsive.

A godly man would recognise that there is a
difference between being attractive and being vulgar.

Milcah the daughter of Saul had physical beauty but a very bad mouth, that punched her husband David's joy, and reduced the day of glory to that which was inglorious. She ridiculed his celebration and dancing before the Lord.

While on another hand the woman he met as a widow, Abigail, brought him only joy for the time he shared with her.

Godly men make effort not to be carried away by the packaging, but what the content is.

They do not pick broken girls.

To keep thee from the evil woman, from the flattery of the
tongue of a strange woman.
Proverbs 6:24 (KJV)

Broken girls become broken wives. What a woman is when single, is what she is likely to be for a long while.

Yes transformed temperaments and enhanced looks, but people do not walk away from the personality they once had. Whatever you pick is what you live with, and if you picked her purely for beauty you will very soon realise that the inner qualities must not be overlooked.

In like manner also, that women adorn themselves in modest
apparel, with shamefacedness and sobriety; not with broided
hair, or gold, or pearls, or costly array;
But (which becometh women professing godliness) with good
works.
Let the woman learn in silence with all subjection.
1 Timothy 2:9-11 (KJV)

A broken girl who has not found healing may be the start of the wrong generation.

The attempt is not to condemn a woman but to know that, if you commit your life to such relationship you might be marrying a *V.D.P.* - a very draining person. In fairness, some of us may be attracted partly because the marriage may have been intended by God to be an assignment.

Some of the people today who are blessing the world and touching lives come from a background of incredible hurt, pain, abuse, molestation, and yet with time, have found healing and made progress.

They avoid demanding to touch, test and taste.

Marriage is honourable in all, and the bed undefiled: but whoremongers and adulterers God will judge.
Hebrews 13:4 (KJV)

This book is about godly men, men who apply wisdom that is from above and not the cunningness that has become popular with our time.

In these days of libertinian values, and at such times when men are encouraged by the press to look like Adonis in order to conquer more. When sexual prowess is used to measure the greatness of men. In contrast is the Word of God which challenges the believer and the Christian man to control his passion.

If you are in a relationship with a lady, godly wisdom demands that you treat her like your sister, honour her as a lady, and do not take advantage of her.

Define the scope and the extent of the relationship, do not heat the oven if you are not going to be cooking. And in conclusion, raise the standard of your relationship with the opposite person.

Wise men are careful in the use of the phrase "I love you".

Let love be without dissimulation. Abhor that which is evil; cleave to that which is good.
Romans 12:9 (KJV)

Men and women process information differently. A man receives information primarily with the left side of his brain, the side of logic, before comparing it with the right, the side of emotion.

A woman is totally different, she receives with the side of her emotion and checks it out with the side of logic.

When a man says "I love you", and is probably using it in a general term, the woman receives such statements spirit, soul and body. She interprets the word from the point of emotion.

It is important that as a man who honours women, you are careful about the use of the word, even when you mean the God kind of love.

Wise men avoid idealism in marriage, not expecting a Proverbs 31 woman.

Likewise, ye husbands, dwell with them according to knowledge, giving honour unto the wife, as unto the weaker vessel, and as being heirs together of the grace of life; that your prayers be not hindered.
1 Peter 3:7 (KJV)

The day after you both say "I do", wise men must learn to move away from being married to an ideal wife and facing the real situation in which they have found themselves.

We all have ideal spouses somewhere in our minds before we say "I do", what they should look, talk, and behave like.

Men do not want women to change, they want the woman they married to stay the way they found her. Women on the other hand want the man to change. As a matter of fact they make efforts to change the man.

In order to move away from idealism you need to learn to live in the house you have built; live with what you have found.

One man built on a Rock, the other built on the sand. When the elements came, they both stood by the consequence of what they built. The Bible says to be happy with the wife of your youth.

Drink waters out of thine own cistern, and running waters out of thine own well.
Let thy fountains be dispersed abroad, and rivers of waters in the streets.
Let them be only thine own, and not strangers' with thee.
Let thy fountain be blessed: and rejoice with the wife of thy youth.
Let her be as the loving hind and pleasant roe; let her breasts satisfy thee at all times; and be thou ravished always with her love.
Proverbs 5:15-19 (KJV)

The mirror of the woman in Proverbs 31 is great, her industry, commitment, love, respect and subsequent honour she brings to her family.

You must recognise the sociology of today's family and the challenge the woman faces having to go to work to supplement her husband's income. In the light of that fact, honour your wife by not making unnecessary or unrealistic demands.

Remember, God said He would make a helpmeet for Adam, a woman is a helpmeet. In other words an appropriate helper that meets the standard of the man. But remember also, that if she is a help, the original responsibility belongs to the man.

Wise men avoid the trap of comparing a partner with their mother or sister.

The responsibilities of a woman are already cumbersome and challenging.

First she comes in as a wife, then she realises she has other jobs to do; she becomes your counsellor; the mother of your children; she cooks; runs the home, in some cases runs the domestic budget; balances the account; takes care of the house.

Comparing her with your mother or your sister, whether positive or negative, would be unfair on her. Maybe if it is on a positive level it becomes a source of inspiration.

Comparison weakens a person's confidence if it is negative. Always remember, your wife looks up to you for validation and encouragement.

Wise men are real, they refuse to walk in what they are not.

Let love be without dissimulation. Abhor that which is evil;
cleave to that which is good.
Romans 12:9 (KJV)

The test of your wisdom may be your ability to operate in honesty; honesty they say is the best policy.

Always remember to provide things honest in the sight of God and man.

Wise men are also real and in the reality of their person they walk in humility, always remembering to be a mirror of what Christ is.

Remember, now that you are born-again you have a new identity, you are a new man, and what used to be the measure of a man is no longer the ruler by which you measure your life.

In the Kingdom of God, the true measure of a man is not to esteem himself more than he should.

Wise men do not impress women with their dreams, visions and goals without marital intentions.

And now it is true that I am thy near kinsman: howbeit there is a kinsman nearer than I.
Tarry this night, and it shall be in the morning, that if he will perform unto thee the part of a kinsman, well; let him do the kinsman's part: but if he will not do the part of a kinsman to thee, then will I do the part of a kinsman to thee, as the LORD liveth: lie down until the morning.
Ruth 3:12-13 (KJV)

Some men are very slippery and unable to make a very clear commitment to a relationship. I call the disease they are suffering from "commitment phobia". It is as if their commitment to one lady will end their life.

The root of the matter may be that they would no longer enjoy the attention from various females which they once attracted.

The man who is walking in the wisdom of God would realise that he should not use a carnal means to impress women and hope to achieve a spiritual end.

So let your yes be yes, do not give the wrong impression. Hear from God clearly, before you commit yourself to a relationship or begin to share too intimately and always ask yourself what Jesus would do in the same situation.

They do not exaggerate their past experiences.

But what things were gain to me, those I counted
loss for Christ.
Yea doubtless, and I count all things but loss for the
excellency of the knowledge of Christ Jesus my Lord: for
whom I have suffered the loss of all things, and do count
them but dung, that I may win Christ,
Philippians 3:7-8 (KJV)

Pride goes before a fall; humility is the mark of great men.

A godly man who is wise would remember that if he must glory, it should be in the fact that he knows the Lord and not to celebrate how sordid his past was, but how grateful he is to God for finding him and saving him from the power and penalty of sin.

Wise men are frank about their health and finances.

Recompense to no man evil for evil. Provide things honest in the sight of all men.
Romans 12:17 (KJV)

Remember that scripture again "providing things honest in the sight of God and man".

The price of falsehood is too high, it is important as a godly and wise man to pursue honesty at all times.

Be honest about the state of your affairs, and about your health. If you are in a relationship or are going into one, look for the person who will accept you as you are. Know that life should not be measured by the abundance of the things you have.

It is better to be vulnerable than to hide facts that may come back to haunt you in the future.

They do not expect too much too soon.

The majority of the first part of this book addresses the godly and wise man in his relationship with the person of the opposite sex.

Remember that if you are in a relationship, you do not hide things, you do not also hasten things, you let them unfold as the time goes on. In general, learn the power of patience. Good things come to he who is patient enough to wait for the Lord to cause it to happen.

Be diligent and pursue the vision God has put in you.

Wise men do not go after women for conquests or boast about them.

Likewise, ye husbands, dwell with them according to knowledge, giving honour unto the wife, as unto the weaker vessel, and as being heirs together of the grace of life; that your prayers be not hindered.
1 Peter 3:7 (KJV)

The principles shared in this book have to do with the pursuits of the "New Man", who has been renewed by the finished work of Christ.

Therefore if any man be in Christ, he is a new creature: old things are passed away; behold, all things are become new.
2 Corinthians 5:17 (KJV)

A man who walks in wisdom is not caught boasting about his female conquests. To do that would be to reduce relationships to that which is beastly.

Animals are the only ones who are not commanded to control their passion, that probably is the reason why mating only comes in seasons and at those seasons, any fellow beast of the opposite gender will do.

Walk right, but also live right. Do not take advantage of people who at some point may become vulnerable to you, possibly because of closeness and friendship. Honour the woman God brings to you.

Find new value in being a believer, and treat ladies as joint-heirs together of the grace of life.

Wise men do not underestimate the importance of prayer.

Likewise, ye husbands, dwell with them according to knowledge, giving honour unto the wife, as unto the weaker vessel, and as being heirs together of the grace of life; that your prayers be not hindered.
1 Peter 3:7 (KJV)

Daily Daniel ensured the windows were open as he looked towards Jerusalem and addressed his prayer. Men tried to stop him, they could only fault him on matters of prayer, the very thing they faulted in his life was what got him out of the den of lions.

Do not allow yourself to be carried away by your natural gifting and ability. Understand that it is by kneeling that you conquer.

They are sensitive to the leading of the Holy Spirit.

For as many as are led by the Spirit of God, they are the sons of God.
Romans 8:14 (KJV)

The Holy Spirit is the third person of the Godhead, He is the Executive One who is here to make the mind of Christ known.   He leads, guides, and directs, without Him we would make mistakes, but with Him we would walk in the counsel of the Lord.

A wise man who seeks to pursue godliness will know that the Holy Spirit is the key to spiritual living .

The thief cometh not, but for to steal, and to kill, and to destroy: I am come that they might have life, and that they might have it more abundantly.
John 10:10 (KJV)

This I say then, Walk in the Spirit, and ye shall not fulfil the lust of the flesh.
But if ye be led of the Spirit, ye are not under the law.
If we live in the Spirit, let us also walk in the Spirit.
Galatians 5:16, 18, 25 (KJV)

He is the key to spiritual loving.

....because the love of God is shed abroad in our hearts by the Holy Ghost which is given unto us.
Romans 5:5 (KJV)

The Holy Spirit is the key to spiritual labour.

But ye shall receive power, after that the Holy Ghost is come upon you: and ye shall be witnesses unto me both in Jerusalem, and in all Judaea, and in Samaria, and unto the uttermost part of the earth.
Acts 1:8 (KJV)

He is the key to spiritual leading.

For as many as are led by the Spirit of God, they are the sons of God.
Romans 8:14 (KJV)

He is the key to spiritual looking (sight).

While we look not at the things which are seen, but at the things which are not seen: for the things which are seen are temporal; but the things which are not seen are eternal.
2 Corinthians 4:18 (KJV)

Never rely on impulse or hunches to lead you. Your life is too precious to base major and minor decisions on strong impressions.

They are wise not to seek counsel from just anybody.

Where no counsel is, the people fall: but in the multitude of counsellors there is safety.
Proverbs 11:14 (KJV)

The scriptural passage quoted talks of a multitude of counsellors. In other words, consulting many hearts and examples, whether dead or alive is like gathering various pollen from different flowers to make the honey in the honeycomb.

Your exposure will qualify your explanation. How you are able to expose and expound a truth is dependent on the number of people who have been your teachers.

But be very wise, not everybody qualifies to be your counsellor. Make your pastor your friend and your counsellor. Seek wisdom from those who know better than you, read their books, study what they have documented.

It is no use spending forty years to learn what another man has captured in his book after his own forty years experience.

Wise men do not double-date.

But have renounced the hidden things of dishonesty, not walking in craftiness, nor handling the word of God deceitfully; but by manifestation of the truth commending ourselves to every man's conscience in the sight of God.
2 Corinthians 4:2 (KJV)

The Christian man must always remind himself that he is a new man. The old lifestyle of craftiness in dealing with the opposite sex must not continue. Such style dishonours God.

Scripture teaches the believer to abstain from all appearances of evil. Double-dating is walking in such appearance.

Always remember that you are a man of God, and that title is not only for those who are full-time in ministry. It is for men who have been called to worship and serve the Lord Jesus Christ.

Keep a clear conscience because you want to provide things honest. Keep a sensitive conscience, so that you are easily convicted even in the things that did not seem clearly ungodly to you.

Do not handle the Word of God deceitfully, it often leads to justifying one's position in the things that are not right.

In your relationship with the persons of the opposite sex, whether in your own marriage or an intended one, you should remember you are dramatising the marriage of Christ and His church, do not add to the script what Jesus would not do.

They do not argue for a dead relationship to continue.

They say "let sleeping dogs lie". The problem with the prostitute which Solomon dealt with, was that she was not prepared to lay to rest a child that was already gone.

Many times people hold on to issues as if they are fresh. Do not hold on unnecessarily if the lady says it is time to call it a date. You might be tampering with her destiny and hindering yourself too.

Seek God to hear Him clearly and if He says it is over seek Him to find your own catharsis and healing. Some people do not find it easy to come out of a relationship. Ask the Lord to heal you enough to build a genuine and open friendship with this person without having to walk in animosity.

Pray for God's divine leading in the future and while you are at it, do not get into relationships out of a rebound. A rebound is when you quickly jump into relationships in order to cover up or make up for the one which just ended. You need to heal properly before another.

Wise men do not play with a woman's emotions.

Let love be without dissimulation. Abhor that which is evil;
cleave to that which is good.
Romans 12:9 (KJV)

If you will not cook why are you heating the oven?
We said earlier on that there should be a
commitment, and if there is none, to define the
relationship so that the lady knows clearly that it is
not intended to end up in marriage.

If you play with a woman's emotion you are sowing
a seed, and the harvest may be disastrous. The
scriptures teach us to walk in love, that is void of
hypocrisy.

To play with a woman's emotion and be hypocritical,
the scripture calls it evil.

Wise men are men of their word, they do not make empty promises.

Finally, brethren, whatsoever things are true, whatsoever things are honest, whatsoever things are just, whatsoever things are pure, whatsoever things are lovely, whatsoever things are of good report; if there be any virtue, and if there be any praise, think on these things.
Philippians 4:8 (KJV)

The quality of a man's life is in direct proportion to the integrity and quality of his word. You are only as good as your word, if your word is not good, you are not good.

So the Bible says you are to be a man of a honest report. Your words should always portray honesty.

The carriage of evil report is the abortion of your own destiny.

The ten men who brought an evil report concerning Caanan in the days of Moses joined every adult who left Egypt and destroyed their destiny.

As a godly and wise man do not promise what you cannot deliver, be honest enough to admit your limitations.

God is good because His Word is good. Let your word be good enough. Keep to the times you said you will come, and if you are being delayed make it known on time, and remember, do not lie!

Lie not one to another, seeing that ye have put off the old man with his deeds;
Colossians 3:9 (KJV)

They do not give women an ultimatum to make a decision to marry them.

For as many as are led by the Spirit of God, they are the sons of God.
Romans 8:14 (KJV)

It is safe to conclude that as a man who pursues wisdom and the will of God, you are concerned that the woman you will share your future with knows the Holy Spirit and His leading.

If God is to guide her into decision-making, then allow her to receive independently from Him without coaxing, coercing or giving ultimatums.

We are all children of God and we have access to our Father to receive from Him. Albeit, it is according to our level of reception and understanding of the leading of the Holy Spirit. Do not put the lady under pressure and because you have waited for so long does not mean you cannot wait further.

Lastly do not blackmail a lady to accept your proposition, if she is not comfortable you wait, if you know that it is of God. Eventually it will all turn out according to God's purpose.

And we know that all things work together for good to them that love God, to them who are the called according to his purpose.
Romans 8:28 (KJV)

They do not gamble with a woman's future.

You may be gambling with a woman's future if you hang around her for so long without a commitment.

You may be gambling with a woman's future if you are seen all the time with her, even though you have no commitment to her.

You may be gambling with a woman's future if along with your indicated intentions to marry her, you are also doing the same with somebody else.

You may be gambling with a woman's future if you are using her for other reasons, as in the case of people who live in countries where marriage could mean settling their immigration problem.

You could be gambling with a woman's future if you use her as a breadwinner or for your economic advantage.

Wise men do not use women for selfish ends.

Likewise, ye husbands, dwell with them according to knowledge, giving honour unto the wife, as unto the weaker vessel, and as being heirs together of the grace of life; that your prayers be not hindered.
1 Peter 3:7 (KJV)

Beneath the expressed reason for relating to a woman may be the unspoken. If your intentions for being around a woman is only for your own purpose, you must remember that you are sowing a seed and a full harvest will follow.

It is a selfish end when a woman is used by you to satisfy your ego, to prove your sexual prowess or to settle your immigration problems.

You may be using a woman for selfish ends, if she is just one more collection among many things you feel you own.

They do not speak to a woman without praying and seeking God's face.

Then shall we know, if we follow on to know the LORD: his going forth is prepared as the morning; and he shall come unto us as the rain, as the latter and former rain unto the earth.
Hosea 6:3 (KJV)

And the LORD said, I have surely seen the affliction of my people which are in Egypt, and have heard their cry by reason of their taskmasters; for I know their sorrows;
And I am come down to deliver them out of the hand of the Egyptians, and to bring them up out of that land unto a good land and a large, unto a land flowing with milk and honey; unto the place of the Canaanites, and the Hittites, and the Amorites, and the Perizzites, and the Hivites, and the Jebusites.
Exodus 3:7-8 (KJV)

The pursuit of God to know His mind concerning a relationship could only result in a clear understanding. Why? Because Jehovah sees what you are going through and what the future is.

Jehovah hears your cry, prayer and knows your fears.

Jehovah knows what is best for you and is able to make it happen for you.

Jehovah leads particularly those who leave the choice to Him.

The pursuit of God will bring a revelation of what God's mind and intention is for your future. Be the first to know what you ought to do by reason of the leading of God.

Wise men do not fudge issues.

Finally, brethren, whatsoever things are true, whatsoever things are honest, whatsoever things are just, whatsoever things are pure, whatsoever things are lovely, whatsoever things are of good report; if there be any virtue, and if there be any praise, think on these things.
Philippians 4:8 (KJV)

Their yes is yes, and their no is no. You know where you stand with the godly and wise man. He is not a man of two faces and not the one who does not mean what he says.

They do not overlook danger signs.

For as many as are led by the Spirit of God, they are the
sons of God.
Romans 8:14 (KJV)

I was born in the northern part of the country of
Nigeria, where vultures were known to dominate its
skies, flying anywhere cows migrate. They come
down when a cow dies, the closer the cow is to
death, the lower the flight of the hawk and vulture.

How can a man know if a relationship is dying?

It may be over if she is constantly avoiding you.

It may be over if every time she promised to come,
or whenever you said you were coming, your
presence was always met with her absence.

It may be over if your calls are not returned.

It may be over if in moments of discussion she can
no longer look at you face to face but has to respond
to you with her back turned.

It may be over if you are getting snappy answers for revealing questions.

It may be over if she is now amnesiac about previous agreements and arrangements.

They avoid communicating the problem they experienced in the hand of spiritual leaders with the lady.

Saying, Touch not mine anointed, and do my prophets no harm.
1 Chronicles 16:22 (KJV)

God has given His church leaders to help us.

And he gave some, apostles; and some, prophets; and some, evangelists; and some, pastors and teachers;
Ephesians 4:11 (KJV)

They were intended to be our guides, our priests to show us the light and help us grow into manhood in Christ.

Leaders are humans prone to mistakes and we are also prone to place them on pedestals they may not measure up to. When that happens we get disappointed?

Remember earlier we said a woman receives information with the right side of her brain, the side of emotion. If you discuss leaders, or other believers, she is not likely to overlook such information in her future relationship with them as you might be able to do.

Discussing leaders negatively with your fiancée or wife is sowing a bad seed that will produce a dangerous harvest.

You may be ruining her confidence in that leader, you might also find yourself exposing your wife to negative issues she is likely to internalise.

But if you build the lady's esteem of leaders, she will be able to look up to him/her for counsel next time you both sit before the leader. You might need that leader in the future.

You might have enough maturity to disregard what you know or have heard of him/her, your spouse may not be.

Recognise the calling of God on your pastor, the Christian leader or fellow believers and appreciate the grace of God in their lives.

Wise men receive healing from broken relationships.

For if there be first a willing mind, it is accepted according
to that a man hath, and not according to that he hath not.
2 Corinthians 8:12 (KJV)

Good things sometimes end. Relationships come to
an end and it is not only the woman who feels the
impact of a broken relationship.

Many times the man too may find his self-esteem,
understanding and conviction totally shattered.
Particularly where a lot of emotional investment has
been made.

As a man who is led of God and wants to walk in
wisdom, when such happens remember to draw from
the grace of God. When things fall do not fall with
them.

First of all develop a bounce back method by
learning to draw from what the Word of God says
concerning relationships.

Secondly, always know it is not over until it is over. This relationship may be over but life is not.

This relationship may be over, but all relationships are not.

Yes, your heart is broken but the body has been designed by God to heal itself and the One who made you can reach into the very depth of your spirit and bring healing.

Pray and seek the help of the Holy Spirit as you do so.

Likewise the Spirit also helpeth our infirmities: for we know not what we should pray for as we ought: but the Spirit itself maketh intercession for us with groanings which cannot be uttered.
And he that searcheth the hearts knoweth what is the mind of the Spirit, because he maketh intercession for the saints according to the will of God.
Romans 8:26-27 (KJV)

They avoid making approaches for fun.

Marriage is a matter of destiny, it is the coming together of two people to share their lives to begin a beginning and possibly raise children who start a new generation.

It is too salient and too sacred a thing to be approached lightly.

Marriage is in my opinion for adults, and adulthood is not a matter of natural age, but maturity; all round maturity.

They do not shower women with what they cannot afford.

Diamonds they say are a woman's best friend. They also say that women like the best things in life. But in general and in due honesty it is not so.

In general, most women want a happy home where things work, where there is laughter, joy and comfort. Relationships built on such qualities would last longer.

As a godly man be modest in everything you do. It is wise and best to even show less than you earn or have. Let the opposite sex, the woman you intend to marry discover that your true worth is more than you have shown.

Be liberal, but do not brag. Liberality is a sign that you are not stingy. Bribery is an indication that you are buying love. It should not take the Beatles to know that money cannot buy love.

Be honest about what you have, do not go for ladies who want status. Let the relationship you would go into be for who you are in God.

They avoid using gifts, influences, and position to buy affection.

As we have previously said, beware of greek gifts, at least do not give or receive them. Let everything you do have a valid and clear reason.

Of course, surprises should exist in your relationship with a woman, but such gifts must be tied to the expression of love and to the celebration of special occasions and events. They must not be in order to impress or to keep.

Do not influence a woman's decision with things you give, learn to provide out of honesty.

Do not use your position, if you lose it tomorrow, love will go out of the window.

Godly men avoid talking about marriage before relationships are built.

Marriage is honourable in all, and the bed undefiled: but whoremongers and adulterers God will judge.
Hebrews 13:4 (KJV)

I assume that the majority of men who would read this book are people who are regular in a church fellowship.

On occasions when relationships have started within the context of local churches, it is as if things move so fast and there is almost no time to clarify where a relationship is. It is important to avoid misunderstanding in the future.

Firstly, you need to date a lady properly and if you are convinced there is something to the relationship as you seek God's face and watch your relationship, move on to court the lady properly. Beyond that, let there be the occasion when there is an engagement and if it is God's perfect will, let it end at the altar where you both say I do.

Wise men do not make a woman confirm their expectations.

Some men will carry themselves in a way that is obviously petty and childish. They would like to see a woman confirm their expectation.

They suspect she loves them, they think she wants to go out with them and instead of clarifying in their minds if this is God and if not to make efforts to indicate that there could not be anything to it. They begin to pursue the lady until she confirms their expectation; that she is interested in them.

As a godly and a wise man, remember that you are different, and a woman's confirmation of your expectation may only tickle your ego and reveal your immaturity.

They do not make suggestive or lewd statements.

Let no man despise thy youth; but be thou an example of the believers, in word, in conversation, in charity, in spirit, in faith, in purity.
1 Timothy 4:12 (KJV)

You are a man of God and like Paul wrote to Timothy; a young pastor who found himself in a challenging city called Ephesus, you must be an example in the words you speak.

Let your words lift, let it impart grace to the hearers. Let a dying man find help in listening to you.

Let a sick person find healing because of the word that proceeds from your mouth.

Remember that the words Jesus spoke are spirit and life. Follow the example of your Master.

They are wise enough to admit their mistakes.

Be of the same mind one toward another. Mind not high things, but condescend to men of low estate. Be not wise in your own conceits.
Romans 12:16 (KJV)

Call a spade by its proper name. Those who cover their sin will not find forgiveness.

When you are confronted with the errors and mistakes you have made in the management of your life, godliness and wisdom is shown not in the denial or avoidance of it, but in finding what the problem is, facing and finishing it.

Refuse to allow Satan to use it to condemn you.

Be vulnerable, let some trusted people know when you have fallen into error, so they can help you to find your footing back.

Micah would say:
Rejoice not against me, O mine enemy: when I fall, I shall arise; when I sit in darkness, the LORD shall be a light unto me.
Micah 7:8 (KJV)

Be vulnerable, let the Word of God work in you. Have a heart so tender the Holy Spirit can convict you. Refuse to hide your past so that it does not come back to condemn you.

Why? because sin condemns, then it kills.

If you are relating to the opposite sex you need to let such person know you are not superman. You are simply a sinner whose sins have been forgiven, and have now become a new person.

You are not sinless, God is teaching you daily to break the grip and power of sin. Admit that you are not without mistakes, you are just learning daily to live the victorious life.

They have learnt to treat women with the ultimate respect.

The elder women as mothers; the younger as sisters, with all purity.
1 Timothy5:2 (KJV)

Timothy who was sent to pastor a church in Ephesus, was here being encouraged by Paul to regard elder women as mothers and the younger sisters with respect and purity.

When you come into relationship with a woman, choosing that person from the sea of humanity and calling the person your spouse will now mean to honour her. She is now your wife, and deserves honour from your mother, family and sisters.

Show her due honour and not play down her achievement. If you play down a woman's achievement because you want her to feel less, you have not found your true value outside of your status.

Let the woman you have chosen to be your partner,
be the person you can help to even improve her
productivity. Help her to gain confidence and to
feel comfortable among her friends, because you
have built her self-esteem.

Wise men in relationships make it great fun.

Whom having not seen, ye love; in whom, though now ye see
him not, yet believing, ye rejoice with joy unspeakable and
full of glory:
1 Peter 1:8 (KJV)

Today's actions are tomorrow's history. If the lady you court would one day become your wife, the dating, courtship, engagement and wedding date becomes the story you must tell over the years.

What kind of memory would you like to have?

What kind of picture would you like to give your children?

So if you are single and are reading this, prepare to spoil the lady you meet. Truly give her treats like a lady.

Let there be breaks when both of you share your vision, look into the future and talk of the days and the things you will build together.

If the relationship ends in marriage, keep courting her. Talk every day. Talk intimately; talk in details. You never know what you share with her from the depth of your heart might one day be your protection if something were to rise against your home.

Wise men seek to build friendship and respect for a girl's family.

And they said, We will call the damsel, and enquire at her mouth.
And they called Rebekah, and said unto her, Wilt thou go with this man? And she said, I will go.
And they sent away Rebekah their sister, and her nurse, and Abraham's servant, and his men.
Genesis 24:57-59 (KJV)

When you walk in wisdom, it would not take you too long to recognise the fact that the princess you met must have been raised by a family that made her look the way she is.

A family raised the person whom today you call your fiancée or your wife as the case may be.

It is important if you are single to know that you do not just get married to a lady, you marry a family. If her relations are opposing your courtship and subsequent marriage, make effort to explore a mutual agreement.

Do not go to the altar without exploring every possible avenue. Eighty five per cent of opposed relationships, particularly by parents, never seem to work.

Qualify the kind of opposition. If it is outside of the revealed will of God and the standard of the Word of God, it should not bother your mind.

If parents are opposing because you come from different cultures or races, that is not a strong ground. But recognise the benefit of parental consent, where it is possible to get it.

Whether you have marital bliss or trouble will be determined by the efforts you put in to see that everyone is carried along.

Wise men do not keep ladies out for unreasonable hours.

The night is far spent, the day is at hand: let us therefore cast off the works of darkness, and let us put on the armour of light.
Let us walk honestly, as in the day; not in rioting and drunkenness, not in chambering and wantonness, not in strife and envying.
But put ye on the Lord Jesus Christ, and make not provision for the flesh, to fulfil the lusts thereof.
Romans 13:12-14 (KJV)

We have earlier indicated that your relationship with your spouse or the lady who will be your wife, must be like that of Christ and His church. Therefore it is to be God-glorifying.

Wisdom will make a man not to stay late in a woman's house.

*The night is far spent, the day is at hand: let us therefore
cast off the works of darkness, and let us put on the armour
of light.*
*Let us walk honestly, as in the day; not in rioting and drunk-
enness, not in chambering and wantonness, not in strife and
envying.*
*But put ye on the Lord Jesus Christ, and make not provision
for the flesh, to fulfil the lusts thereof.*
Romans 13:12-14 (KJV)

As a single man who is intending to glorify God
with everything he does, one of the key areas where
your Christian testimony can be manifest is your
choice to not keep a lady awake or stay too long in
her house, or her in your house.

Firstly, because all things must be done to the glory
of God, and if anything you do brings disrepute, the
believer needs to watch out.

When you stay late in a woman's house it is hard to
witness to the neighbours who may think that the
same things they would have done when they are

alone is what you are likely to be practising.

Such late hanging around is hard to explain to people who do not know how you are able to control your life and walk in purity.

If the world disbelieves you, even an angel cannot be the best witness in your favour.

People are bound to draw wrong conclusions for many things the believer does. It is wise to see that you walk in a way that shows decorum and integrity.

They do not put themselves in a compromising situation.

Wherefore, my brethren, ye also are become dead to the law by the body of Christ; that ye should be married to another, even to him who is raised from the dead, that we should bring forth fruit unto God.
For when we were in the flesh, the motions of sins, which were by the law, did work in our members to bring forth fruit unto death.
Romans 7:4-5 (KJV)

The believer is not called to walk in isolation, but to be insulated. To live in the world but not belong to it.

Having said that it is important to know places that may just be wrong and not helpful to your testimony. It is important to know relationships that would be regarded as compromising situations.

Unnecessary closeness, particularly to unsaved persons may make them draw conclusions and perpetuate rumours which are unhelpful to your testimony. You do not want to become a victim of blackmail.

Moreover the Lord's Name is at stake, and everything must be done to honour it.

Sometimes believers find themselves like Joseph, trapped, maligned and falsely accused. If such is the case, God will always provide a way of escape.

They avoid playing macho man.

Wherefore, brethren, look ye out among you seven men of honest report, full of the Holy Ghost and wisdom, whom we may appoint over this business.
Acts 6:3 (KJV)

Muscle size, biceps and physical looks are used today to measure the ultimate man. Mr. Universe is not rated because he is the most acceptable, righteous or holy. Today's strongest man is not honoured for his credibility or integrity, but his physical strength.

Godly men know that what honours God is not their physical strength, though bodily exercise has its profit.

Your boast must be in the Lord, and not in your strength. Samson's power was not in his physique, if it were Delilah would not have asked. It is in the fact that he was anointed. Your boast also must be that you are led by the Spirit of God and you manifest the fruit of the Spirit and not physical strength.

They admit and never deny who they are.

Paul described himself as the "chief of sinners".

Gideon said he was "the least of his father's house".

David confessed "in sin did my mother conceive me".

Solomon the wisest man said, "I need wisdom to lead this your great people".

Godly men are not afraid to admit their weaknesses, they are not afraid to seek help.

Wise men are not afraid of a commitment.

Commitment is different from involvement, when you are involved with a thing, it only costs you a little. Commitment means giving everything it takes to make it work.

Two things were involved in a typical English breakfast. The chicken laid the egg, yet it survived because it was involved. The pig donated the bacon, it died, that is commitment.

Wise men avoid physical and verbal abuse.

The man by nature cannot match a woman in the number of words he is able to process and communicate his feeling. Yet some men have found that in the attempt to handle pressure in their relationship with the opposite sex, they have ended up being verbally abusive.

A wise man will recognise the need to speak in a way that honours the Lord, and honours ladies.

Remember that your words are to be seasoned, they should communicate grace. Words that do not condemn but bring healing to those who hear you.

Godly and wise men are men of covenant.

*And it came to pass, when he had made an end of speaking
unto Saul, that the soul of Jonathan was knit with the soul of
David, and Jonathan loved him as his own soul.
And Saul took him that day, and would let him go no more
home to his father's house.
Then Jonathan and David made a covenant, because he loved
him as his own soul.
And Jonathan stripped himself of the robe that was upon him,
and gave it to David, and his garments, even to his sword,
and to his bow, and to his girdle.
1 Samuel 18:1-4 (KJV)*

The ability to keep covenant is a distinguishing
factor of godly men. David's commitment to
Jonathan made him to extend the keeping of the
covenant to Mephibosheth years after Jonathan's
death.

While on Jonathan's part, his commitment made him
to be willing to protect David against his father's
anger.

The successful man lives under the reality of God's watchfulness.

Oh that I were as in months past, as in the days when God preserved me;
Job 29:2 (KJV)

For the man of God, the mark of success is the ability to trust God's watchfulness and not to put his confidence in the protection he is able to buy for himself. Remember that God will take care of you.

Learn at all times to rely on God, and not your physical strength or macho-ness. Always understand that you cannot move away from God's presence if you must enjoy His protection.

The successful man enjoys God's protection.

Oh that I were as in months past, as in the days when God preserved me;
Job 29:2 (KJV)

One of the most powerful passages on God's protection and care for the believer is Psalm 91. This is assumed to be a psalm of Moses because it has no title and the previous one was written by him. Often times the previous psalm with a name indicates who wrote the subsequent one.

Leading the children of Israel through the wilderness for forty years, Moses must have known the power of God's protection.

Surely he shall deliver thee from the snare of the fowler, and from the noisome pestilence.
He shall cover thee with his feathers, and under his wings shalt thou trust: his truth shall be thy shield and buckler.
Thou shalt not be afraid for the terror by night; nor for the arrow that flieth by day;
Nor for the pestilence that walketh in darkness; nor for the destruction that wasteth at noonday.

A thousand shall fall at thy side, and ten thousand at thy right hand; but it shall not come nigh thee.
Only with thine eyes shalt thou behold and see the reward of the wicked.

Psalms 91:3-8 (KJV)

The successful man increases in his confidence and trust that God is able to protect him. He does not put his trust in man.

Operating in divine revelation.

When his candle shined upon my head, and when by his light
I walked through darkness;
Job 29:3 (KJV)

Divine revelation is the key to Biblical understanding. You can study theology and every tool for understanding the Bible, but Jesus' Word indicates that it has to be revealed to you.

And Jesus answered and said unto him, Blessed art thou, Simon Barjona: for flesh and blood hath not revealed it unto thee, but my Father which is in heaven.
Matthew16:17 (KJV)

Jesus said furthermore that only revealed truth saves,

And ye shall know the truth, and the truth shall make you free.
John 8:32 (KJV)

That again indicates that revealed truth sets free.

Divine revelation gives you access to the things that cannot be naturally processed from merely reading the Word of God. It helps you to have access into the purpose of God, as revealed by His Word but discerned by His Spirit.

*I was in the Spirit on the Lord's day, and heard behind me a
great voice, as of a trumpet,*
Revelation 1:10 (KJV)

The successful man operates in divine direction.

When his candle shined upon my head, and when by his light
I walked through darkness;
Job 29:3 (KJV)

You cannot be full of God and be led by impulse. The scripture does not say "as many as are led by impulse, hunches, premonition or feelings".

It is important to pursue the leading of God, it is important also to be able to discern when God is speaking.

Leaving the leadership and direction of your life to the Holy Spirit is the mark of maturity.

For as many as are led by the Spirit of God, they are the
sons of God.
Romans 8:14 (KJV)

Walks in the counsel of the Lord on all matters.

As I was in the days of my youth, when the secret of God was upon my tabernacle;
Job 29:4 (KJV)

The counsel of the Lord is another way to describe the revealed will of God. You cannot afford to be led by the philosophies of the world because they keep changing.

Ideas come and go, what was propounded today may be rejected tomorrow. It is important to seek God's will.

Making the Bible the final authority in your life distinguishes you as a man after God's will. A man who makes the counsel of the Lord his final authority may be misunderstood by men, but in the end the counsel of the Lord will stand, and it will speak better things.

Blessed is the man that walketh not in the counsel of the ungodly, nor standeth in the way of sinners, nor sitteth in the seat of the scornful.

But his delight is in the law of the LORD; and in his law doth he meditate day and night.

And he shall be like a tree planted by the rivers of water, that bringeth forth his fruit in his season; his leaf also shall not wither; and whatsoever he doeth shall prosper.

Psalms 1:1-3 (KJV)

The reality of the presence of the Lord is with him.

When the Almighty was yet with me, when my children were about me;
Job 29:5 (KJV)

One of God's covenant Names revealed in Ezekiel is Jehovah Shammah, which means, "the Lord is there".

It was round about eighteen thousand measures: and the name of the city from that day shall be, The LORD is there.
Ezekiel 48:35 (KJV)

The presence of the Lord brings power.

Living in His presence exposes one to unlimited joy, power and peace.

There is a dimension of fulfilment that cannot be known except in His presence.

The godly man pursues the presence of the Lord and makes effort to keep it once it is gained.

Manifesting heaven's prosperity.

When I washed my steps with butter, and the rock poured me out rivers of oil;
Job 29:6 (KJV)

The purpose of Biblical prosperity is to establish covenant with God, and to carry out His purpose.

But thou shalt remember the LORD thy God: for it is he that giveth thee power to get wealth, that he may establish his covenant which he sware unto thy fathers, as it is this day.
Deuteronomy 8:18 (KJV)

It delights God, it pleases Him to prosper the believer, spirit, soul and materially:

Beloved, I wish above all things that thou mayest prosper and be in health, even as thy soul prospereth.
3 John 1:2 (KJV)

It has nothing to do with struggles, it is a provision already made by Christ's vicarious death.

For ye know the grace of our Lord Jesus Christ, that, though he was rich, yet for your sakes he became poor, that ye through his poverty might be rich.
2 Corinthians 8:9 (KJV)

And God is able to make all grace abound toward you; that ye, always having all sufficiency in all things, may abound to every good work:
2 Corinthians 9:8 (KJV)

The man made successful by God will access it by applying himself to the word of God, eventually manifesting the God kind of success:

This book of the law shall not depart out of thy mouth; but thou shalt meditate therein day and night, that thou mayest observe to do according to all that is written therein: for then thou shalt make thy way prosperous, and then thou shalt have good success.
Joshua 1:8 (KJV)

The successful man taps into God's abundance.

When I washed my steps with butter, and the rock poured me out rivers of oil;
Job 29:6 (KJV)

Needs would never stop in a world that is perpetually placing demands upon the believer. The godly and successful man knows that the promise of God to him is abundance:

The thief cometh not, but for to steal, and to kill, and to destroy: I am come that they might have life, and that they might have it more abundantly.
John 10:10 (KJV)

Access into what God has already provided will have to be by walking in hourly obedience.

If ye be willing and obedient, ye shall eat the good of the land:
Isaiah 1:19 (KJV)

Tapping into God's abundance is necessary in order to be a promoter of the work of the Kingdom; to be a blessing to your generation; and to be a blessing to your family.

Promotion and leadership.

When I went out to the gate through the city, when I prepared
my seat in the street!
Job 29:7 (KJV)

For promotion cometh neither from the east, nor from the
west, nor from the south.
But God is the judge: he putteth down one, and setteth up
another.
Psalms 75:6-7 (KJV)

The scripture quoted earlier mentions east, west, and
south, but not the north. The Lord sits on the side
of the north and promotion will come from Him.

The godly man knows that when it is his time and
season for him to be elevated, no man can stop it,
because it comes from God.

Walking in dominion.

When I went out to the gate through the city, when I
prepared my seat in the street!
Job 29:7 (KJV)

The successful man knows that his ordination,
calling and mandate is that of dominion.

And God said, Let us make man in our image, after our
likeness: and let them have dominion over the fish of the sea,
and over the fowl of the air, and over the cattle, and over all
the earth, and over every creeping thing that creepeth upon
the earth.
So God created man in his own image, in the image of God
created he him; male and female created he them.
And God blessed them, and God said unto them, Be fruitful,
and multiply, and replenish the earth, and subdue it: and
have dominion over the fish of the sea, and over the fowl of
the air, and over every living thing that moveth upon the
earth.
Genesis 1:26-28 (KJV)

Since the fall of man, his environment and
experience has created a man with dysfunctions, but
what we regain in Christ is the ability to walk in the
fullness of what we were ordained for.

Being clothed with honour and glory.

The young men saw me, and hid themselves: and the aged arose, and stood up.
Job 29:8 (KJV)

The godly man is clothed with honour and glory because he is an extension of the Kingdom of God.

God does it firstly by His finished work of salvation, secondly as He cleanses our hearts with the blood of Jesus, thirdly as He makes the love of Jesus spread abroad in our heart, and lastly as His Word gives us a sense of understanding that we are God's people, we begin to manifest the beauty and honour of His glory.

A man of honour and respect.

The young men saw me, and hid themselves: and the aged
arose, and stood up.
Job 29:8 (KJV)

A godly and successful man is known by the honour upon his life. Honour is more valuable than money.

The Bible says, "a good name is to be sought more than silver and gold".

A godly man knows that when he has finally been able to command the respect and honour of his colleagues, nothing could be more valuable than it.

Honour is the glory of kings and it is maintained by learning to walk in hourly obedience to the Lord. Honouring the Lord in everything that you do.

.

Enjoying divine elevation.

The princes refrained talking, and laid their hand on their mouth.
Job 29:9 (KJV)

The godly and successful man knows that his promotion is from God.

For promotion cometh neither from the east, nor from the west, nor from the south.
But God is the judge: he putteth down one, and setteth up another.
Psalms 75:6-7 (KJV)

Heaven's favour rests upon his life.

Thou shalt arise, and have mercy upon Zion: for the time to favour her, yea, the set time, is come.
Psalms 102:13 (KJV)

Mordecai was not known for the money he owned or wealth he commanded. Honour was upon his life at home and in due season he was elevated by God.

The mark of a godly man is that, his day of promotion is not orchestrated by him, but God makes the connection.

Walking in the glory that silences the voices of nobles.

The nobles held their peace, and their tongue cleaved to the roof of their mouth.
Job 29:10 (KJV)

God operates in glory, He lives in glory, and He wants His people to walk in it and to manifest it.

The glory that comes from above is greater than being born in nobility. The nobles see the hand and grace of God, and honour it.

Walking in the glory that silences the mouth of the critical.

The nobles held their peace, and their tongue cleaved to the roof of their mouth.
Job 29:10 (KJV)

Joe was the pastor of the church within his community. It was a sad day when the police announced to him "You are under arrest for abuse and murder".

A little child had been killed, abducted from the gate of the school where Joe had gone to drop his daughter and was the last person to be seen speaking to the girl.

The police interrogated Joe's wife and asked her "Would your husband have done this?" She looked into the dark distant skies, all of the years she spent with him, rushing through her mind, and as if in one second she found the answer, she responded with an emphatic no!

It will be months later before Joe would remember

further details about the most incriminating piece of evidence.

He had loaned his torch light, which bore his initials, to a vagrant who was always hanging around the church. Now, this torch light had been found beside the girl's body and was the suspected murder weapon.

It was then that another witness recalled seeing this vagrant near the school on the day of the murder.

Joe's wife casting of doubt on the evidence, and her ability to testify for her husband, helped in the arrest of the culprit.

A godly and wise man lives a life which does not confirm evil report, or confirm rumours, and as people come close, they see a man who walks in glory.

The testimonial of a successful man provokes blessing from other people.

When the ear heard me, then it blessed me; and when the eye saw me, it gave witness to me:
Job 29:11 (KJV)

Many more people are blessed by your blessing, nobody ever increases by your lack except the devil.

Your blessing helps you to leave an inheritance for your children.

The presence of a successful man commands divine and natural approval.

When the ear heard me, then it blessed me; and when the eye saw me, it gave witness to me:
Job 29:11 (KJV)

Everything around Abraham increased and multiplied because of his pursuit of God and his confidence in God.

He believed God and it was counted unto him for righteousness. He prospered and even his nephew who hung around him prospered.

God blessed the house of Potiphar because of Joseph who lived with him.

A godly and wise man automatically provokes the blessing of the Lord.

The mark of a successful man is not how much he has, but how much he does for others.

*Because I delivered the poor that cried, and the fatherless,
and him that had none to help him.*
Job 29:12 (KJV)

Jesus came to seek and to save that which was lost.

*For the Son of man is come to seek and to save that which
was lost.*
Luke 19:10 (KJV)

In His incarnation, He did not *per se* portray just natural wealth, rather His glory was in the fact that He came to save mankind.

Job became a father and helper to those who lacked help.

Because I delivered the poor that cried, and the fatherless,
and him that had none to help him.
Job 29:12 (KJV)

Make every waking moment, every new day an opportunity to touch the people around you, to minister to those who do not have the same privileges and opportunities.

True success is measured by your ability to reach out and minister to those who are broken around you.

True religion is to visit the fatherless.

Pure religion and undefiled before God and the Father is this,
To visit the fatherless and widows in their affliction, and to
keep himself unspotted from the world.
James 1:27 (KJV)

Is not this the fast that I have chosen? to loose the bands of
wickedness, to undo the heavy burdens, and to let the
oppressed go free, and that ye break every yoke?
Is it not to deal thy bread to the hungry, and that thou bring

the poor that are cast out to thy house? when thou seest the naked, that thou cover him; and that thou hide not thyself from thine own flesh?
Isaiah 58:6-7 (KJV)

True success reaches out to those who are perishing and rescues them.

The blessing of him that was ready to perish came upon me:
and I caused the widow's heart to sing for joy.
Job 29:13 (KJV)

C. T. Studd was one of the Cambridge Seven; a group of young men who upon their graduation from the elite university decided to dedicate their lives to God and to reach the less fortunate. It was a commitment to preach the gospel of Jesus Christ.

C.T. Studd in his own words said he would rather live in a corner in a hut in Africa, than to be in the best of cities and to be out of the will of God.

That is the perspective of a successful man.

True success makes a man put a new song in the mouth of the widow, and joy in the heart of such.

The blessing of him that was ready to perish came upon me:
and I caused the widow's heart to sing for joy.
Job 29:13 (KJV)

For close to forty-two years, George Mueller dedicated his life to helping orphans, by building one of the most successful Christian run orphanages in Bristol.

In those years he trusted God to feed the children, and without a bank account to his name, he put a smile on the face of many children. Not one day, did he and the children ever go to bed without food in their stomach.

That is the mark of a godly and successful man.

True success can be measured by what you are daring enough to do: launch a new business, go to college, start physical training, learn a new language or change a career in mid-life.

If a man die, shall he live again? all the days of my time will I wait, till my change come.
Job 14:14 (KJV)

In his mid sixties, T.L. Osborne the world evangelist declared that he was willing and ready to learn the French language in order to reach more people with the glorious good news of Jesus Christ.

Success and a clear vision of it, would mean not giving up; giving in; or giving out; until the battle is won.

Job's success was not compromised by unrighteousness but measured by the quality of righteousness.

I put on righteousness, and it clothed me: my judgment was as a robe and a diadem.
Job 29:14 (KJV)

Abraham believed God and it was reckoned unto him for righteousness.

He staggered not at the promise of God through unbelief; but was strong in faith, giving glory to God;
And being fully persuaded that, what he had promised, he was able also to perform.
And therefore it was imputed to him for righteousness.
Romans 4:20-22 (KJV)

Hezekiah refused to bow to the gods of Sennacherib, and though he was ridiculed by Sennacherib and his soldiers, his stand for righteousness was vindicated by God who rose to fight for him.

You do not lose by standing for righteousness, and though you may suffer temporary setback by those who hate what you stand for, you will in the end have a testimony that you have honoured the Name of the Lord.

Success for Job was in the amount of justice he brought for others.

I put on righteousness, and it clothed me: my judgment was
as a robe and a diadem.
Job 29:14 (KJV)

Three men walked past the man who was attacked on his journey from Jerusalem to Jericho.

The priest and the Levite walked on the other side of the road, possibly afraid that he might be dead and did not want to be defiled by touching a dead man.

The Samaritan reached forth, helped him, touched him, set him free, set him on his feet and launched him into a future.

When we bring joy to those who lack it, healing to the hurting and peace to troubled people.

That is what success is all about.

True success may be measured by the amount of eyes we have enlightened.

I was eyes to the blind, and feet was I to the lame.
Job 29:15 (KJV)

The philosophy of our world has changed. We pay those who kick a bag of wind around a stadium, monies that are so difficult to quantify. While the people who gave us our first taste of education are sometimes the most under-appreciated and under-paid.

Do not measure your success only by your financial gains, but by the number of lives you have been able to touch, by the number of people whose darkness you have turned to light and for whom you have brought brightness and a smile back to their face.

Success is determined by the number of people you have given mobility.

I was eyes to the blind, and feet was I to the lame.
Job 29:15 (KJV)

Many things incapacitate and make people lame. Mental lameness, financial, physical, spiritual and emotional crippleness.

A godly and successful man makes himself available for God to use to touch, to heal, to set free from any form of lameness and give back mobility, where it had been taken.

Success indeed will be measured by the number of the helpless and poor whom you have given a new testimony.

I was a father to the poor: and the cause which I knew not I searched out.
Job 29:16 (KJV)

Jim Elliott was a young man who turned his back on everything called the American Dream to go and minister to the Auca Indians of the Amazon jungles. Questioned by his friends who knew how brilliant he was,and the wisdom of going to live his life among these people who do not know him, who do not appreciate him, though he had a prospect of being outstanding in his chosen field in his own country.

His response was "a man is no fool who gives up what he cannot keep to gain what he must not lose". Jim Elliott was killed by the same Auca Indians whom he had gone to minister to.

Was he a loser? Not at all, his widowed wife stayed among those people to minister, and many came to know the Lord.

Success is not to be measured by just the natural, but by the people who we have given a new testimony.

Successful people make other people's matter their cause.

I was a father to the poor: and the cause which I knew not I searched out.
Job 29:16 (KJV)

Martin Luther King could have stayed in the confines of his comfortable church in Atlanta Georgia. But the burden of the downtrodden, the sadness of racial discrimination would not let him.

He spoke and reached out, until his dream was snuffed out by a sniper's rifle.

Today his dream is still alive, as others have run with it. But what made him successful and a godly man was not only his ability to expound scripture but taking other people's cause and making it his.

Success is learning to clip the wings of those who progress by wickedness.

The Bible says if you know to do good and fail to do it, you are walking in unrighteousness.

When Jesus stood in the porch of the temple, He spoke so strongly against every manifestation of hypocrisy and wickedness, even though it provoked the hatred of the Pharisees of his days.

But woe unto you, scribes and Pharisees, hypocrites! for ye shut up the kingdom of heaven against men: for ye neither go in yourselves, neither suffer ye them that are entering to go in.
Woe unto you, scribes and Pharisees, hypocrites! for ye devour widows' houses, and for a pretence make long prayer: therefore ye shall receive the greater damnation.
Matthew 23:13-14 (KJV)

Progress in life can be measured by helping the helpless and delivering the hopeless.

And I brake the jaws of the wicked, and plucked the spoil out of his teeth.
Job 29:17 (KJV)

The Samaritan who reached out to the man who was dying by the wayside was hated by the man who he was reaching to minister. He was hated by the man who he was trying to help.

His motivation must be the fact that he understands that success and progress in life is not to be measured by his ability or what he owned, but by the people to whom he brought healing.

The home of the successful is surrounded with the God kind of peace.

Then I said, I shall die in my nest, and I shall multiply my days as the sand.
Job 29:18 (KJV)

People argue from the point of their dysfunctions, and make it seem like everyone must repeat the pain they have been through.

I remember the testimony of my friend who testifies that in all the years of his marriage, there has been no argument. That is possible, particularly because my friend must have built with possible storms and troubles in mind, and therefore laid the foundation for a successful marriage by ensuring that it is built upon the Rock called the Word of God.

So when the storms, the rains, and the floods came, the house was untouched. Peace abounded where there should have been trouble.

That is the mark of success.

Longevity and increase of days is the blessing of the God kind of success.

Then I said, I shall die in my nest, and I shall multiply my days as the sand.
Job 29:18 (KJV)

God's promise for the believer is health, long life, and not to lie in the bed of languishing.

The account of men and women who walked with God in Scripture was that of a long life, a life of healing and health. Abraham, one hundred and twenty years, Moses, one hundred and twenty years.

It is time for you as a godly man to tap into the blessing which awaits you.

When a man is made successful by God, his root of progress will spread.

Jonathan Edwards, a seventeenth century preacher, has been made popular by his message "Sinners in the hand of an angry God". A message delivered after three days of waiting on the Lord. So powerful was it, that his members thought that hell had opened its mouth.

But Jonathan Edwards' godliness and success, is not to be measured by the strength of that message, but the fact that his family three hundred years on is still producing lawyers, accountants, preachers and in 1991 I was privileged to host one of his distant family.

Dr. Leland Edwards, who was in our church on the occasion, was the son of missionaries to Latin America. He also served in Latin America and at the time of his visit to London, his son was also serving as a missionary in Latin America.

He was accompanied on his visit by his grandson who also had the intention of becoming a missionary.

Three hundred years on people from the family of Jonathan Edwards are still making progress in the things of God.

That is a godly man.

Success for those who are blessed by God commands a continuous favour, even in the night season.

I know a man who never ceases to amaze me. All of his adult life was expended to serving the Lord in various capacities until he went full-time, serving the Lord, and quitting his business.

When he retired at close to seventy, the amazing thing was that those he had blessed through his ministry, now turned around to sow more seed into his life that now accounts for more than whatever income or salary he earned when he was gainfully employed and in full-time ministry.

The measure of godly breakthrough is the presence of godly glory.

A man who is after the will of God and who wants to portray godly success, must himself know that nothing beautifies like the presence and the glory of the Lord.

When glory departs from a family, as declared by the wife of one of the sons of Eli when she called her son Ichabod; the result is death, destruction, falling, and danger.

The measure of a godly man is the amount of glory around his life.

Victory in battle attends the life of a man made to succeed by God.

The Scripture does not guarantee that the believer would not face battles.

> *Many are the afflictions of the righteous: but the LORD*
> *delivereth him out of them all.*
> *Psalms 34:19 (KJV)*

But it is in the womb of his battle that victory will be born.

Success attends the effort of a man who is after the will of God. David fought many battles but it was those battles that also qualified him for the blessing of the Lord.

A friend of mine who had gone through the pain of divorce, leaving him a child who was only a few months old. Today he pastors one of the largest churches in the world and makes more impact around the world beyond his city, because of the understanding that "battle surrounds the birth of every miracle".

All men choose to listen to the man blessed by God.

There are men who may never run for office, stand in the town hall to dictate the politics of a nation. But true and godly men are men who because of the grace and blessing of God upon their life, others must come to attention and listen to what they have to say.

In the afflictions and pain of Job, he still commanded the attention of his generation.

A man made successful by God receives his counsel from the Lord.

Unto me men gave ear, and waited, and kept silence at my counsel.
Job 29:21 (KJV)

David said:

Blessed be the LORD my strength, which teacheth my hands to war, and my fingers to fight:
Psalms 144:1 (KJV)

Bezaleel, the sculptor and artist who made all of the special equipment used in the temple, was taught in his night season by revelation.

Jehoshaphat received counsel from the Lord as to how to face his enemy and finish them.

True godliness and true success is, learning not to do what comes naturally, not to take the counsel of men as final, but to know the mind of the Lord on all matters.

When God gives you success, the words of your mouth are enough education.

After my words they spake not again; and my speech dropped upon them.
Job 29:22 (KJV)

There are two men who never cease to amaze me. One of them flows with such wisdom that is difficult for you to write whenever he teaches, Mike Murdoch.

The depth of wisdom which flows from him is obviously by reason of constant listening to the Holy Spirit and the quality of time spent in the presence of the Lord.

A man who loves wisdom so much he built a room for it. Who craves to know and is willing to learn from the simplest of men.

The second man is the man who brought the word "purpose" alive. Myles Munroe.

Dr. Munroe has challenged all mankind to understand that to be without purpose is to be without life.

Godly men know that there is power in words, but not empty words.

Wisdom is the principal thing; therefore get wisdom: and with all thy getting get understanding.
Proverbs 4:7 (KJV)

Even the pain caused by a man lifted by God seems to be a source of education by those who respect him.

And they waited for me as for the rain; and they opened
their mouth wide as for the latter rain.
If I laughed on them, they believed it not; and the light of my
countenance they cast not down.
Job 29:23-24 (KJV)

Mentors speak in a way that is likely to hurt. Your colleagues see your present position; your mentor sees your future.

Your colleagues like you the way you are, your mentor sees what you will become.

Your colleagues endorse your weakness; your mentor works to see it changed.

A godly man who pursues the God kind of success knows that men may be assigned to his life who speak to him, and provoke him to succeed.

John the Baptist called the people who came to hear him, the generation of vipers. Yet they came back again and again.

Joy and favour multiplies for the man who makes others to succeed by his success.

If I laughed on them, they believed it not; and the light of my countenance they cast not down.
Job 29:24 (KJV)

The only qualification of the men who came to David when he found his solace in the cave called Adullam, were dregs, drop outs, debtors, and distressed men.

David was himself a product of a dysfunctional home. Deeply hurt by a lack of parental love and despised by his brothers, found solace in seeking constantly after God.

He dragged men with himself to the presence of God where he found success.

A couple of years later when we read of these men, they were wealthy enough to contribute the substantial part for the building of the temple.

They had become men whose works were now productive.

True godliness and success is not just succeeding in isolation, but touching other lives.

Promotion, honour and leadership is a fruit of the success from God.

I chose out their way, and sat chief, and dwelt as a king in the army, as one that comforteth the mourners.
Job 29:25 (KJV)

As we come close to the appearance of our Lord and Saviour Jesus Christ, we will still hear a few more voices boomerang through the silence of our generation.

Men who will experience a sudden promotion, honour and elevation to the place of leadership. They may be from the clay hills of Virginia or the dark continent of Africa.

They will take the world by surprise and make the mind of the Lord known.

True success is when God takes a minus and makes a plus. When God gives you a sudden elevation when men least expect it.

When you are made successful by God, you will reign in the midst of your brethren as a king.

*I chose out their way, and sat chief, and dwelt as a king in
the army, as one that comforteth the mourners.*
Job 29:25 (KJV)

"The dreamer cometh", his brothers cried, as Joseph
showed up in the horizon bringing food for his tired
brothers.

They plotted, they schemed, they finally agreed
either to kill him, drop him in the well or concluded
to sell him to their cousins.

Twenty years later, on the other end of the table, sat
a man of great regal presence; a man who had every
portrayal of nobility. His brothers bowed to him,
unknown to them, that this was Joseph whom they
sold.

And so when God gives the word that He would
raise and promote, character assassination and the
plottings of men cannot stop the godly success that is
divinely originated.

Those who are lifted by God bring comfort to the ones who mourn in Zion.

I chose out their way, and sat chief, and dwelt as a king in the army, as one that comforteth the mourners.
Job 29:25 (KJV)

What is the source of your success? What is the source of your blessing? How can it be measured? Whose tears have you wiped today? Who will go to bed a better person today? How many souls have you directed and pointed to Calvary?

It is giving your life to point men to Calvary, showing them the finished work of Christ that truly makes you godly and successful.

A man made successful by God develops the skill for managing adversity.

And he said unto me, My grace is sufficient for thee: for my strength is made perfect in weakness. Most gladly therefore will I rather glory in my infirmities, that the power of Christ may rest upon me.
Therefore I take pleasure in infirmities, in reproaches, in necessities, in persecutions, in distresses for Christ's sake: for when I am weak, then am I strong.
2 Corinthians 12:9-10 (KJV)

Understand that you need God's grace to be able to face certain adversities.

If you draw from the grace of God, you would not go down with adversity like common men would do.

True success is the ability to maintain hope against all hope.

*I know that thou canst do every thing, and that no thought
can be withholden from thee.*
Job 42:2 (KJV)

Against all hope, Abraham believed in hope. The
ability to still be hopeful in hopeless situations marks
out godly men who end up being successful.

As Paul stood in a broken ship, he declared to those
with him in the predicament, "there shall be no
loss", having been visited by an angel of the Lord.

*And now I exhort you to be of good cheer: for there shall be
no loss of any man's life among you, but of the ship.*
Acts 27:22 (KJV)

Surrounded by imminent danger, yet confident that
the One who spoke cannot lie.

Godly men do not deny the reality of hopeless
situations, but they see the finger of God and His
ability to deliver the righteous, even in the oddest
of situations and they conclude "it's not over, until
it's over".

Genuine success adds the ability to receive ministry from others.

Then came there unto him all his brethren, and all his sisters, and all they that had been of his acquaintance before, and did eat bread with him in his house: and they bemoaned him, and comforted him over all the evil that the LORD had brought upon him: every man also gave him a piece of money, and every one an earring of gold.
Job 42:11 (KJV)

What a man does not know is often used as a weapon against him.

People's vulnerabilities are explored in the world in which we live, yet the mark of a godly man who pursues the God kind of success is the ability to celebrate the greatness of other people.

Celebrate the wisdom others have which you lack. Make yourself a student of what they know.

Genuine success will add to you the grace to allow others to mentor you.

Mentoring is not only done by people above us. It is downward, lateral and upward.

Somebody knows something you do not know. Somebody has insight into law, which you do not have.

A person has the knowledge of accountancy which can save you from financial or tax blunders.

You do not know everything and it is not a crime to be ignorant in certain areas. Matter of fact, the law of harness requires that you focus on few areas and maximise what you have from there. It states:

"The demand you put on a thing determines what it releases to you. The greater the pressure, the greater the output."

Allow others to mentor you in the area of your ignorance, that way you add to your success and favour.

A truly successful man knows when to stay quiet and show his wisdom by silence.

O that ye would altogether hold your peace! and it should be your wisdom.
Job 13:5 (KJV)

Silence cuts off the fuel that energises the enemy. It sends confusion to the mind of the enemy. If you cannot give a soft answer, God will tell you to stay silent.

A soft answer turneth away wrath: but grievous words stir up anger.
Proverbs 15:1 (KJV)

Silence protects your focus. Your words can be used in evidence against you. Silence cannot be quoted or misquoted.

Your goal is to finish well. Your enemy's goal is the abortion of your destiny.

Those who hate you will not invest money, time, energy and effort to understand you. The Pharisees were always trying to quote or misquote Jesus.

Silence is the answer because your enemy wants to confuse you.

Silence is the best weapon if the root of the attack is envy.

Wrath is cruel, and anger is outrageous; but who is able to stand before envy?
Proverbs 27:4 (KJV)

Your words can stop good relationships.

Whoso keepeth his mouth and his tongue keepeth his soul from troubles.
Proverbs 21:23 (KJV)

Your words will decide the season you are in, qualify who hears your opinion and advice.

Speak not in the ears of a fool: for he will despise the wisdom of thy words.
Proverbs 23:9 (KJV)

If you must speak, it should be for deliverance.

The words of the wicked are to lie in wait for blood: but the mouth of the upright shall deliver them.
Proverbs 12:6 (KJV)

Silence is the answer, or your words might become a trap.

A fool's mouth is his destruction, and his lips are the snare of his soul.
Proverbs 18:7 (KJV)

The motive behind peoples actions should indicate if you are to be silent or talk.

If you must talk it is only when you use your mouth as a giant killer, champion,and restorer of dreams. Your mouth is a weapon of deliverance, and motivation.

Maturity of your success is seen by your choice to be happy in the face of sadness.

If I say, I will forget my complaint, I will leave off my heaviness, and comfort myself:
Job 9:27 (KJV)

Ecclesiastes 3:4 says *"there is a time to mourn, but there is also a time to be happy"*.

Problems do not last forever. A godly man must know how to manage stress, distress, worry, and trouble.

He must know how to look at things from God's perspective and not be carried away by today's philosophy.

Remember the way of the world is different from how to follow Christ. We must learn to do things from how the natural man would do it.

In the face of adversity count your blessings. When

the enemy shows you the things that are not working for you, remind yourself of the things the Lord has done for you.

Play in your mind the picture of previous victories. Like David, recount the days you brought down the bears and the lions and as you do that today's Goliath will pale and become insignificant.

A man's success is shown in his tendency to make major moves only from strength and not his weakness.

David had two Goliaths he had to deal with. One was King Saul who suggested that his weapon be used both to protect and to fight Goliath, as David went to confront the giant.

For David it was an untested weapon, an unexplored territory, and a land he had never conquered. The irony of it is, if it had worked so well for Saul, how come Goliath was still standing?

At such times when David would confront a battle he had never faced before, the best possible thing a godly man must do is to approach the next battle from the point of his strength and not his weakness.

Do not talk down what God can do in your life.

Do not play down His ability.

Remind yourself that you can do all things through Christ.

I can do all things through Christ which strengtheneth me.
Philippians 4:13 (KJV)

Encourage yourself with the truth that you have been given everything you need that pertains unto life and godliness.

Blessed be the God and Father of our Lord Jesus Christ,
which according to his abundant mercy hath begotten us
again unto a lively hope by the resurrection of Jesus Christ
from the dead,
To an inheritance incorruptible, and undefiled, and that
fadeth not away, reserved in heaven for you,
1 Peter 1:3-4 (KJV)

Go to war you would win.

The measure of Job's success is seen in his pursuit of purity.

I made a covenant with mine eyes; why then should I think
upon a maid?
Job 31:1 (KJV)

Like Job in the scripture quoted, a man must make covenant with his eyes. The enemy takes advantage of men's visual weakness.

The fact that we process a lot of information from how we see it. We are attracted to the opposite sex. The enemy can use that gate to bring in filth, pornography and lewdness.

At the time when kings went to war, David looked at Bathsheba for too long.

The first look was probably a look of admiring, but from beholding, he went to holding, and from holding, it became belonging.

Godliness and your pursuit of success must mean that when you are confronted with such challenge, ask for grace to walk away from it. But it must first start with a quality decision to walk away and to pursue purity.

A man who puts a high price on wisdom will truly walk in ultimate success.

No mention shall be made of coral, or of pearls: for the price of wisdom is above rubies.
The topaz of Ethiopia shall not equal it, neither shall it be valued with pure gold.
Job 28:18-19 (KJV)

In that one dream that changed Solomon's life forever, he was asked what he would want God to do for him. The only one thing he asked was wisdom to rule God's people. With that wisdom came other blessings.

Many years down the road he argues that "wisdom is the principal thing".

Get wisdom, get understanding: forget it not; neither decline from the words of my mouth.
Forsake her not, and she shall preserve thee: love her, and she shall keep thee.
Wisdom is the principal thing; therefore get wisdom: and with all thy getting get understanding.

Exalt her, and she shall promote thee: she shall bring thee to honour, when thou dost embrace her.
She shall give to thine head an ornament of grace: a crown of glory shall she deliver to thee.
Proverbs 4:5-9 (KJV)

True success is the ability to see the testimony beyond the test, the glory beyond the gutter, the get-to beyond the ghetto.

But he knoweth the way that I take: when he hath tried me, I shall come forth as gold.
Job 23:10 (KJV)

The imagination in your heart of your desired destination can ignite the fire to get you out of the most difficult situations.

Jesus kept before Him, the picture of the glory set before Him. As a result he endured the cross, despising the shame.

Daniel painted before himself and his friends, the benefit of not eating the king's vegetable. He ended up as Prime minister of Babylon.

A man walked through the graveyard and fell into an open grave because it was dark. Every effort he made to come out was futile. He gave up, hoping that the following day somebody would come trying to bury someone in the grave.

As he sat in the corner, a drunk stumbled into the same deep grave. The drunk also tried and could not get out, but just when he was going to settle down, he heard a voice from the corner that said, "you can't get out". I tell you, the drunkard did!

Success God's way comes by tenacious pursuit of God.

The way of a fool is right in his own eyes: but he that hearkeneth unto counsel is wise.
Proverbs 12:15 (KJV)

Lose yourself in His presence. Pursue Him in fasting and prayer. Become known for ultimate and total devotion. Deny yourself of good food and good rest. Steal away from human contact to be with God.

Seek His face, then you will get what is in His hands.

Those who wait on Him, shall mount up, those who wait in fasting and praying shall see results.

Wise men carry their spouses and fiancées along on the needs of a man.

Male and female differences sometimes make us to either compliment or complain about each other. The tragedy of the modern man is that he has been drawn away from the family settings in which older people, uncles and great uncles shared truths with him to prepare him for life.

A Wise and godly man would research things that will help his spouse to know more about his need and how to relate to him.

Below are some of those things a man would wish a woman know and do for a man;

A man needs to hear you appreciate what he knows.

He needs to see you rise totally to the things he calls urgent.

He needs to hear abundant encouragement from a woman.

He needs to hear a woman affirm his goals and vision.

Show your belief in his vision.

Do not take his ability to provide for granted.

Express abundant pride in his person and work.

Talk abundantly of the quality he has that has touched you.

Aim to stimulate his mind, emotion and ego.

Do not just notice his good qualities mention them.

Increase the pleasant memories he has.

Ask about his need and fulfil them.

Mention what he has done to bring joy since you married.

Be the foundation and life member of his supporters club.

Blow the trumpets of his achievements.

Praise him profusely for making efforts at self- improvement toward your marriage.

Encourage him to succeed without pushing him to prove or perform.

Find a loving way to tell him to shave.

Be there to help him keep his focus.

Stop counting his mistakes start treating him as a miracle.

Stay out of the way so he can lead.

Know that when you deny your husband the freedom to lead, he reacts instead of acting.

Light a man's fire with abundant affirmation not criticism.

Allow a man to be the compass to give your family direction.

101 ACTIONS OF A WISE MAN

101 ACTIONS OF A WISE MAN

.